SAMURAI

KNIGHTS

Disclaimer:

The battles in this book are not real. It is fun to imagine. These 2 opponents would never fight each other in real life.

45th Parallel Press

Published in the United States of America by Cherry Lake Publishing
Ann Arbor, Michigan
www.cherrylakepublishing.com

Reading Adviser: Marla Conn, MS, Ed., Literacy specialist, Read-Ability, Inc.
Book Designer: Melinda Millward

Photo Credits: © Nejron Photo/Shutterstock.com, back cover, 16; © Rattiya Thongdumhyu/Shutterstock.com,
cover, 5; © tsuneomp/Shutterstock.com, cover, 5; © LightField Studios/Shutterstock.com, 6; © BrunoGarridoMa-
cias/Shutterstock.com, 9; © ledokolua/Shutterstock.com, 10; © FXQuadro/Shutterstock.com, 12; © Tereshchen-
ko Dmitry/Shutterstock.com, 15; © GraphicsRF/Shutterstock.com, 19, 20; © Gorodenkoff/Shutterstock.com, 19;
© vectortatu/Shutterstock.com, 20; © Robert H. Creigh/Shutterstock.com, 21; ©Album/Alamy Stock Photo, 23;
© draco77vector/Shutterstock.com, 24; © HelloRF Zcool/Shutterstock.com, 25; © Ambartsumian Valery/Shut-
terstock.com, 25; ©World History Archive/Alamy Stock Photo, 27; © Boiko Olha/Shutterstock.com, 29

Graphic Element Credits: © studiostoks/Shutterstock.com, back cover, multiple interior pages; © infostocker/
Shutterstock.com, back cover, multiple interior pages; © mxbfilms/Shutterstock.com, front cover; © MF
production/Shutterstock.com, front cover, multiple interior pages; © AldanNi/Shutterstock.com, front cover,
multiple interior pages; © Andrii Symonenko/Shutterstock.com, front cover, multiple interior pages; © acidmit/
Shutterstock.com, front cover, multiple interior pages; © manop/Shutterstock.com, multiple interior pages; ©
Lina Kalina/Shutterstock.com, multiple interior pages; © mejorana/Shutterstock.com, multiple interior pages;
© NoraVector/Shutterstock.com, multiple interior pages; © Smirnov Viacheslav/Shutterstock.com, multiple
interior pages; © Piotr Urakau/Shutterstock.com, multiple interior pages; © IMOGI graphics/Shutterstock.com,
multiple interior pages; © jirawat phueksriphan/Shutterstock.com, multiple interior pages

45th Parallel Press is an imprint of Cherry Lake Publishing.

Library of Congress Cataloging-in-Publication Data

Names: Loh-Hagan, Virginia, author.
Title: Samurai vs. knights / by Virginia Loh-Hagan.
Description: Ann Arbor, MI : Cherry Lake Publishing, [2019] | Series: Battle royale : lethal warriors | Includes
    bibliographical references and index. | Audience: Grades 4–6.
Identifiers: LCCN 2019003640| ISBN 9781534147669 (hardcover) | ISBN 9781534149090 (pdf) | ISBN
    9781534150522 (pbk.) | ISBN 9781534151956 (hosted ebook)
Subjects: LCSH: Samurai—Juvenile literature. | Knights and knighthood—Juvenile literature.
Classification: LCC DS827.S3 L65 2019 | DDC 952/.025–dc23
LC record available at https://lccn.loc.gov/2019003640

Printed in the United States of America
Corporate Graphics

About the Author

Dr. Virginia Loh-Hagan is an author, university professor, former classroom teacher,
and curriculum designer. She wants to write a story about Japanese American
internment. So, she likes learning about Japanese history, culture, and food. She
lives in San Diego with her very tall husband and very naughty dogs. To learn
more about her, visit www.virginialoh.com.

Table of Contents

Introduction

Imagine a battle between samurai and knights. Who would win? Who would lose?

Enter the world of *Battle Royale: Lethal* **Warriors**! Warriors are fighters. This is a fight to the death! The last team standing is the **victor**! Victors are winners. They get to live.

Opponents are fighters who compete against each other. They challenge each other. They fight with everything they've got. They use weapons. They use their special skills. They use their powers.

They're not fighting for prizes. They're not fighting for honor. They're not fighting for their countries. They're fighting for their lives. Victory is their only option.

Let the games begin!

SAMURAI

Samurai learned from their fathers. Or they went to special samurai schools.

Samurai warriors were from Japan. Japan was divided into different classes. The highest classes were rich. The lowest classes were poor. Samurai were at the top. They were the ruling military class. They helped start **shogunates**. Shogunates were governments controlled by the military. Samurai served **daimyos**. Daimyos are lords. Samurai had power over the government and society. They took power away from emperors and **nobles**. Nobles are royal people.

Samurai were well-trained. They started training at a young age. They learned fighting skills. They learned fighting strategies. They fought on horses. They fought in many wars. They fought over rights to land. They fought against **clans**. Clans are families.

Samurai protected rich landowners. They were **armed** guards. Armed means having weapons. Samurai mainly fought with swords. They always wore short and long swords. Their favorite long sword was the **katana**. Katanas are curved swords. Samurai used bows and arrows. They used spears and poles. They used clubs and chains.

They wore **armor**. Armor is protective body covering. Samurai armor was made of small metal scales on plates. Leather cords tied everything together. Samurai also wore helmets. Their helmets covered their heads and necks. Samurai wore **topknots**. Topknots are hair buns. They're at the top of heads. Samurai shaved their forehead hair. This was to keep cool under their helmets.

Samurai rose to power in the 12th century.
They ruled for over 700 years.

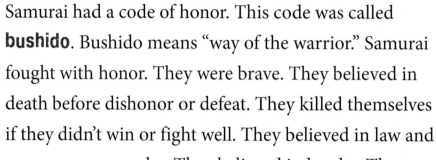

Samurai had a code of honor. This code was called **bushido**. Bushido means "way of the warrior." Samurai fought with honor. They were brave. They believed in death before dishonor or defeat. They killed themselves if they didn't win or fight well. They believed in law and order. They believed in loyalty. They believed in duty. They believed in taking care of their families. They also believed in education. They learned reading and math. They learned about the arts.

Some samurai didn't have masters. They served themselves. They were called **ronin**. Ronin sought revenge. They killed people who dishonored them.

FUN FACTS ABOUT SAMURAI

- An Onna-bugeisha was a female samurai. Female samurai trained. They protected themselves and their homes. They mainly used the naginata. Naginatas are long poles. They have sharp blades at the end.

- Darth Vader is an evil character in *Star Wars*. His helmet is inspired by the samurai helmet.

- Samurai may not have been truly Japanese. Samurai may have come from the Ainu people. Ainu people were natives. They lived in Japan and Russia. They had more hair. They had lighter skin. They had smaller noses. The Japanese treated Ainu people unfairly. But, as samurai, they were very respected.

- The Satsuma Rebellion happened in 1877. It was the end of the samurai. Army soldiers defeated the samurai. There were many more soldiers.

- William Andrews was an English sailor. He was the first Englishman in Japan. He may be the first white samurai warrior. He wasn't allowed to leave Japan. He left behind his English family. He married a Japanese woman.

KNIGHTS

Knights could bring weapons inside a church.
They were defenders of their faith.

Knights fought in **medieval** times. Medieval means Middle Ages. This was from 500 to 1500. During this time, kings ruled. They owned all the land. They gave **fiefs** to nobles and knights. Fiefs are parts of land. In return, nobles and knights served kings. They fought for their kings. Kings paid for all the knights' things. Some nobles bought their own armies of knights.

Nobles passed on their titles to their children. Knights earned their titles. They were called "sirs." Becoming a knight was a way for people to move up. Knights were popular in European countries. They were trained fighters. They started training at a young age. They had warhorses. These horses were big. They were fast. They were strong.

Knights had special training. They were sent to different castles. They learned different skills. They learned to hunt. They learned to ride horses. They learned to fight with many weapons. They mostly fought with swords and shields. Their sword handles were shaped like crosses. Knights learned about religion. They learned to read and write. They even learned to dance.

At first, they served as **squires**. Squires learned from knights. They did chores for knights. They helped knights put on armor. Knights wore **chain mail**. It is a type of armor. It's made from steel rings. Knights also wore full body suits. These suits were made of steel. They hid the face. They covered all body parts. Knights armored their horses as well.

Squires learned how to obey and follow orders.

Knights practiced fighting. They hosted **tournaments**. Tournaments are contests. Knights fought in fake battles. They showed off their skills and talents. They **jousted**. Jousts are ramming games. **Mounted** knights charged at each other. Mounted means riding on animals. Knights used lances. They rammed into each other. They pushed each other off horses. They broke each other's weapons. They also fought on land. They broke teeth and bones. Some knights died. Winners won money and prizes.

Knights had a code of honor. This code was called **chivalry**. Knights believed in defending ladies. They believed in truth. They believed in loyalty. They believed in the church. They believed in helping the poor. They believed in bravery.

FUN FACTS ABOUT KNIGHTS

- There were 2 types of soldiers in the Middle Ages. Knights were one type. The other type were foot soldiers. Foot soldiers were poor. They couldn't afford fancy knights' weapons. They couldn't afford horses. They used farm tools as weapons. They fought on the ground.

- Arbalests are crossbows. They have a special tool. The tool draws back and releases the string. They had good aim. They were quick and easy to use. They were invented in the 12th century. They marked the end of the knights. An arbalest could take down 2 knights a minute from a safe distance. Guns were invented soon after. Knights couldn't compete.

- Medieval castles had spiral staircases. Spiral means to curl around. Spiral staircases were invented for war. They helped defend castles. They stopped knights. Knights had a hard time going up spiral staircases.

- Knighthoods are still given out today. But they're not given for fighting. They're given for good service. For example, Elton John is a singer. He was knighted. He's sometimes called Sir Elton John.

CHOOSE YOUR BATTLEGROUND

Samurai and knights are fierce fighters. They're well-matched. Both groups are from upper classes. Both groups have an honor code. Both groups are trained fighters. But they have different ways of fighting. So, choose your battleground carefully!

Battleground #1: Sea

• Samurai live in Japan. Japan is an **island**. Islands are surrounded by water. Samurai know how to live off the sea. But they don't travel much. They stay in Japan.

• Knights live in Europe. But they travel to different countries. They usually go by land. They travel on their horses. They camp on land. But they also travel in ships.

Many knights fought in the Crusades.
The Crusades were religious wars.

Battleground #2: Land

- Samurai fight to protect their land. They fight to gain land. Most of their fighting is done on land. They can fight on land and on horses.

  - Knights own land. They also serve nobles who have land. They're good fighters on land. They depend on their warhorses. They use horses more than samurai.

Battleground #3: Mountains

- Over 70 percent of Japan has mountains. Its mountains have a lot of forests. This means that samurai are used to fighting on **rugged** land. Rugged means rocky and uneven.

  - Knights have experience fighting in different areas. They'll have trouble getting horses up mountains.

ARMED AND DANGEROUS: WEAPONS

Samurai: Samurai used a tanto. Tantos are short, sharp daggers. Daggers are knives. They're used as weapons. Samurai always carried one or two tantos. Tantos weren't used against swords or spears. They were too short. They were used for slashing. They were used for stabbing. They were used at close range. They were used as a last resort. Samurai mainly used tantos to kill themselves. They cut out their guts. Or they pushed tantos up through their stomachs to their hearts.

Knights: Knights used lances. Lances were long pole weapons. They were used by mounted warriors. They were used to charge into people. They were heavy. So, they weren't good for throwing. They broke upon impact. So, they were only used once. Lances were used with vamplates. Vamplates are small circle plates by the handles. They stopped hands from sliding up. They protected knights during impacts.

FIGHT ON!

The battle begins! Samurai and knights have arrived. They're in an open field. Their leaders talk about the battle rules. They agree on the terms. They form battle lines. They agree to meet in the middle.

Move 1:

Mounted knights line up in the front. They yell, "Charge!" They rush forward. They guide horses using their knees and feet. They raise their shields. They lower their lances.

Move 2:

Mounted samurai archers race ahead. Archers shoot their arrows. They hit the knights. Some arrows hit in between the gaps in their armor. They hit the horses. Samurai keep shooting.

Samurai fought for honor.
Knights fought to win.

Move 3:

Mounted knights ram their lances. They knock off some samurai. Some samurai die from the impact. Lances break apart. Knights throw lances to the ground. They grab the reins of samurai horses. They bring horses back to their base. They take as many horses as possible.

Move 4:

Samurai focus on the knights on foot. Knights thrust out their swords. Knights' swords are longer than samurai swords. But katanas are sharper. Samurai slash away. They can't cut into knights' armor. So, they use their little swords. They stab armpits. They stab hands. They slash with one hand. They stab with the other. They also try to knock off knights' armor.

Samurai learned martial arts. Knights practiced wrestling.

LIFE SOURCE: FOOD FOR BATTLE

Samurai: Rice is a main food dish for Japanese people. Samurai ate a lot of brown rice. Brown rice is more like a grain. Samurai ate simple meals. They had a bowl of rice. They had fish. They had a vegetable dish. They ate fresh and pickled vegetables. They especially liked cabbage. They ate yams. They ate radishes. They ate beans. They ate nuts. They also ate tofu. Tofu is made from mashed soybeans.

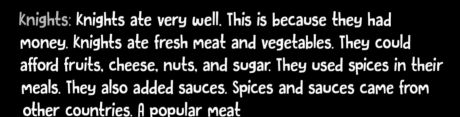

Knights: Knights ate very well. This is because they had money. Knights ate fresh meat and vegetables. They could afford fruits, cheese, nuts, and sugar. They used spices in their meals. They also added sauces. Spices and sauces came from other countries. A popular meat dish was mutton. Mutton is young sheep meat. It was expensive. The meat was tender. Roasted leg of mutton was a favorite.

Move 5:

Knights call other knights to step in line. They move in **formation**. Formation means moving together. Knights move in a straight line. They hold **pikes**. Pikes are long poles with sharp blades. Knights stab samurai with pikes. Mounted knights circle around samurai. They keep them in front of the knights' pikes.

Move 6:

Samurai force knights out of line. They move them all around. They duck from the knights' pikes and swords. They leap. They jump. They can move faster than knights. They tire out the knights. Knights have a hard time breathing in their armor.

Knights were taller than samurai.

AND THE VICTOR IS . . .

What are their next moves?
Who do you think would win?

Samurai could win if:

- They get rid of knights' squires. Knights can't get dressed by themselves.
- They get rid of knights' weapons, armors, and horses. Knights have stronger and more advanced things.

Knights could win if:

- They get samurai to act without honor. Samurai kill themselves if they're dishonorable.
- They learn to fight without armor. Their armor slows them down. It's hard to move with all that gear.

Female knights are called dames.

Samurai: Top Champion

Tomoe Gozen was born around 1157. She was a female samurai warrior. She was brave. She was beautiful. She was a good archer. She was a good sword fighter. She was a good horse rider. She was married to a military commander. She led her own army. She led over 1,000 warriors. She beheaded enemy leaders. She escaped capture. She fought at the Battle of Awazu. Her husband's horse got trapped in a rice field. He was shot with an arrow. He died. Before he died, he begged Gozen to leave him. Gozen refused. She didn't leave his side. She fought against the enemies. She was one of the last surviving warriors. She started her own school for female samurai. She may have become a monk. She was only mentioned in one Japanese story. Some experts wonder if she really existed. Her story inspired many people. She was a great role model for women.

Knights: Top Champion

William Marshal became a knight in 1166. He was like a rock star. Stories were written about him. Marshal was described as the "best knight in the world." He was one of the richest men in England. But he wasn't born rich. At age 12, he was sent to France. He trained to be a knight. He trained for 7 years. His father died and left him no money. So, he made his own money. He was a great fighter. He fought in tournaments. He won a lot of prize money. He fought his way to the top. He served several English kings. He even ruled in the king's palace. He was given land and titles. Nothing stopped Marshal. At age 50, he could scale castle walls. He took out enemies with a single blow. At age 70, he led a battle against French armies. He captured over 500 knights. His last words were, "I cannot defend myself from death."

Consider This!

THINK ABOUT IT!

- How are the samurai and knights alike? How are they different? Are they more alike or different? Why do you think so?
- If the samurai and knights lived at the same time, do you think they would've fought each other? If they did, who would've won? Why do you think so?
- Learn more about ninjas. How are samurai and ninjas alike? How are they different? What would happen if samurai and ninjas fought against each other?
- Samurai and knights had honor codes. What is your honor code? What does it mean to have an honor code? Why are honor codes important?
- What is the role of class in the lives of samurai and knights? What does class mean? How is class used to hurt people? How is class used to help people? Should class matter? Why or why not?

LEARN MORE!

- Gravett, Christopher. *Knight*. New York, NY: DK Publishing, 2015.
- Lee, Adrienne. *Samurai*. North Mankato, MN: Capstone Press, 2014.
- Osborne, Will, Mary Pope Osborne , and Sal Murdocca (illust.). *Knights and Castles*. New York, NY: Random House Children's Books, 2011.
- Tashiro, Osamu. *The Samurai Handbook: From Weapons and Wars to History and Heroes*. New York, NY: Gakken, 2019.

GLOSSARY

armed (ARMD) having weapons
armor (AHR-mur) body covering used as protection
bushido (BUSH-ee-doh) a samurai's code of honor meaning "way of the warrior"
chain mail (CHAYN MAYL) armor that is made of linking metal rings
chivalry (SHIV-uhl-ree) a knights' code of honor that values respect, truth, and loyalty
clans (KLANZ) families
daimyos (DIME-yoz) Japanese lords
fiefs (FEEFS) parts of land given on condition of service
formation (for-MAY-shuhn) a formal arrangement used in military strategies
island (EYE-luhnd) land surrounded by water
jousted (JOUST-id) competed in a contest in which knights ram lances into each other
katana (kuh-TAH-nuh) a curved sharp sword
medieval (mee-DEE-vuhl) of the Middle Ages

mounted (MOUNT-id) riding on an animal
nobles (NOH-buhlz) aristocrats or people with noble births
opponents (uh-POH-nuhnts) groups who compete against each other
pikes (PIKES) long poles with blades at the end
ronin (ROH-nin) a samurai without a master
rugged (RUHG-id) rocky and uneven
shogunates (SHO-guh-nits) governments controlled by the military
squires (SKWIREZ) knights-in-training who serve knights in order to learn about being a knight
topknots (TAHP-nahts) hair buns placed at the top of the head
tournaments (TOOR-nuh-muhnts) contests in which people compete in different games or rounds
victor (VIK-tur) the winner
warriors (WOR-ee-urz) fighters

INDEX